Betrayed
One Woman's Journey

by

Martie Zuckerman

TP

TELEMACHUS PRESS

BETRAYED: ONE WOMAN'S JOURNEY

Cover art and design by Telemachus Press

Cover Art:
Copyright © Thinkstock/F1online/126404484
Copyright © Thinkstock/Photos.com/87754984/© Getty Images/Jupiterimages

Images ©
iStockphoto/2439899/Broken Window/JuneStock
iStockphoto/2580148/Wrath!/knape
iStockphoto/11652400/Sadness/helenecanada
Thinkstock/123692848/Headache/iStockphoto
Thinkstock/57612420/Close-up of the hands of a couple/Stockbyte
Thinkstock/93646675/dark ride/Hemera
Thinkstock/95507959/Prayer/iStockphoto
Thinkstock/96635624/Merging theater masks/iStockphoto

Published by Telemachus Press, LLC
http://www.telemachuspress.com

Visit the author website:
www.timelesswoman.com

ISBN 978-1-937698-94-2 (eBook)
ISBN 978-1-937698-95-9 (paperback)

Version 2012.03.13

Printed in the United States of America
10 9 8 7 6 5 4 3 2 1

A Timeless Woman Publication

This book is lovingly dedicated to my mother, Grace Harvey Wilson.

Betrayed

One Woman's Journey

Table of Contents

Shattered   1
Beliefs   2
Shattered Dreams   3
The Chill   4

Wrath   5
The Volcano   6
Red Roses For A Blue Lady   7
Anger   8

Performances   9
The Actress   10
Coward's Choice   11
Questions   12
Ten Percent   14

Remorse   15
Dances   16
Distortion   17
Silence   18
Changes   19
Memories   20
The Substitute   21

Distrust   23
Patience   24
The Enemy   25
Voices   26

Circles   27
Valleys   28
Devastation   29
No Answers   30

Escape   31
Second Best   32
Stuck   34
The Battlefield   35
Timing   36

Trapped   37
Cycles   38
Dawning   39
Decisions   40
Exposed   41
Friends   42
Forsaken   43
Impatience   44
Impressions   45
Muscles   46
Shifting Sands   47
Starting Over   48
The Debt   49
The Fog   50
The Keeper   51
Unforgiven   52
Visions   53
Wonderful   54
Vanished   56

Forgiveness   57
Accounting   58
New Beginnings   59
The New Chapter   60
Ya, But   61

SHATTERED

Beliefs

I thought my life was a fairy tale,
I believed it was ideal.
I had no idea it was all a sham,
That nothing I had was real!

I didn't know how you mocked me daily
Or how you laughed inside,
Whenever I spoke of our marriage,
And my overwhelming pride.

What a fool I was; what a scapegoat!
Now there's a descriptive word!
I turned a blind eye to your actions
And believed just what I heard.

I believed when you said you loved me.
I believed when you said you were true.
I believed that you respected me;
I believed in us; in you.

Now my beliefs have all been shattered;
I struggle each day to survive.
To make a new life out of rubble;
To keep what's left of my love alive.

Shattered Dreams

My life as I knew it is over!
Things will never again be the same;
Pride in our love and our marriage;
The pleasure of having your name.

You've taken away my comfort,
You've stolen my peace of mind.
Your words now cannot heal me,
No matter how loving and kind.

They are after all just verbiage,
Your actions spoke the truth so clear;
My days are now filled with anger,
Disappointment, remorse and fear!

The Chill

I got used to being by myself;
I learned to be alone.
I got used to being in our "house"
Instead of in our "home."

You got used to other women.
You found joy in other arms.
You found pleasure in their bodies.
You delighted in their charms.

You schemed to be away from me;
You lied about appointments.
Apparently your life at home
Was too filled with disappointments!

You chose to search for something new
Had you grown tired of the old?
You sought the heat of passion
As your love at home grew cold.

WRATH

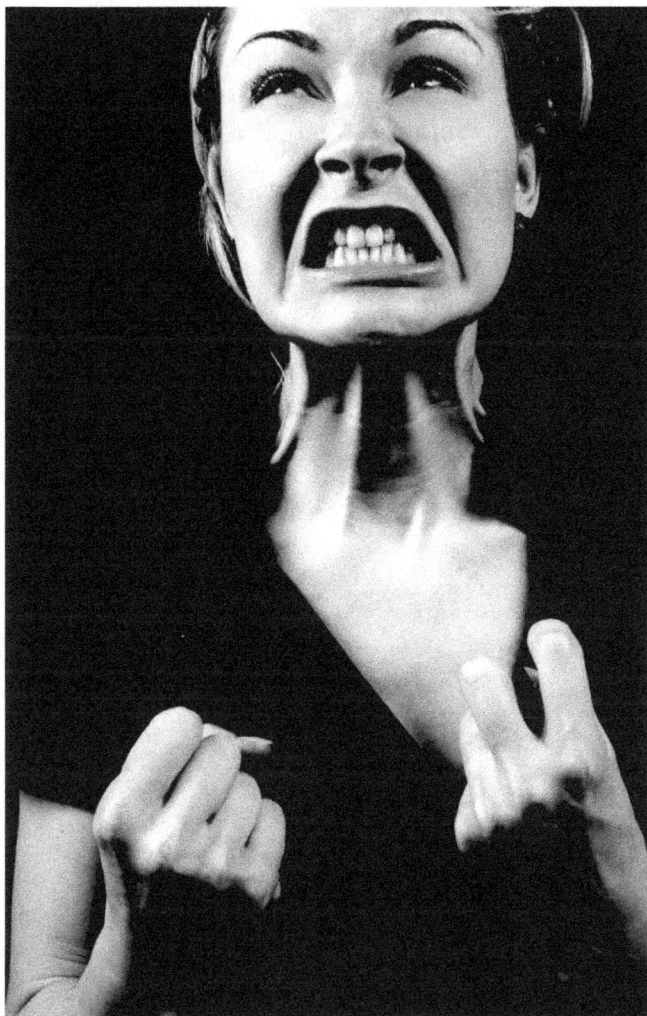

The Volcano

Anger builds within me,
Then boils to the top!
Words best left unspoken
Like lava flow non-stop.

Grief commands my senses;
My mind becomes a cage,
'Til tremors rack my body,
And sobs suppress my rage.

Red Roses For A Blue Lady

Thank you for the flowers!
They'll make everything all right!
They'll make up for all my tears,
For all my sleepless nights!

They'll make up for all your lies;
They'll take away my pain!
I'm sure that they'll sustain me;
Until you cheat again!

There is a poem I didn't write
They're someone else's words;
But here it is, with my new take;
It speaks of love and birds:

"The red rose is a falcon
the white rose is a dove,
The red rose breathes of passion
the white rose speaks of love …"

A falcon is a carnivore that will
Tear my heart to shreds,
While you expend your passion
In other women's beds!

So forgive me if the roses
No longer smell so sweet,
But I can't enjoy their beauty
As I wallow in defeat!

Anger

I get so incredibly angry
I shake with inner rage!
I can't get past your actions,
I just can't turn the page!

I try so hard to move ahead,
I try to leave the past;
But a rage just builds inside me
And escapes in one big blast!

I'm angry because you cheated!
I'm angrier that I've stayed!
I'm angry because I have to pay
For all the mistakes you made!

Somehow it doesn't seem quite fair
That I'm the one to lose,
When you're the one that had the fun;
The one that got to choose.

You deliberately deceived me
For a very, very long time;
There's just no way around it;
I now curse these ties that bind!

PERFORMANCES

The Actress

You destroyed what we had; you're a bastard!
You cast our love aside.
You ignored your vow of fidelity;
You smiled as you lied!

You showed no respect for our marriage.
You decried me as your wife.
You rocked my very foundation;
You attacked my tenet of life!

Now you're "sorry?" You want to start over?
You want me to forgive?
I can't get beyond my anger!
I don't even know how to live!

For years I believed I was special,
Now that's been taken away.
Now I'm just a shell of a woman,
With a lot of roles to play.

Coward's Choice

I wasn't "enough" to keep you at home.
I'll be "less" as I grow older.
What's left of my love is weakening,
As my anger makes me bolder!

Visions are constantly in my head
Reminding me of your trysts.
My heart continues to harden
As my hands clench into fists!

My anger is greater than any remorse
I have because you strayed;
My anger grows as I realize,
That I will probably stay!

I'm here as long as you'll have me,
I'm taking the easy path.
Perhaps one day I'll walk away,
When I tire of this wrath.

But I'll stay as long as I have to.
I'll try to guard my heart.
I'll stay though it's the coward's choice;
Not the one that's smart!

Questions

Why did you ever marry me?
Were you afraid of being alone?
Was I an easy solution;
Better than an empty home?

Did you need a live in helper?
Someone to always care?
Was I just better than nothing?
Someone to always be there?

When did you realize you'd blown it?
When did regret set in?
When did you decide that to cheat on me
Wouldn't be a sin?

Did you feel you'd done your duty,
So to roam would be okay?
Did you think I'd never figure it out,
If you cheated during the day?

Did you enjoy speaking about her?
Did my jealousy add to the thrill?
Did you tell her you needed her body heat
Because I'd developed a chill?

Did the two of you laugh at my failures?
Did you plan for my trips away?
Did you pass the nights with her in mind
Waiting for the light of day?

I think I know you'll never change
And I'll always be too "much!"
The question is; do I stick around;
Knowing I'm just a crutch?

Ten Percent

Grasp the roles available;
Overcome the strife.
Go to work; perform your job
Be a loyal wife!

Accept the new reality;
Suppress the inner rage.
Smile a lot; act the part;
Remember; life's a stage!

Give up your dreams; let them go;
Accept there is no hope!
The past is past; it can't be changed!
It's time to learn to cope!

The fairy tale is over!
Reality is at the door!
The time has come to settle;
You mustn't look for more!

Take just what you are given,
Be grateful for the tithe;
Swallow your words; dry your tears;
Move along with life!

REMORSE

Dances

Please hold on to any regret you feel,
Don't let it disappear.
If your memories are painful,
Always keep them near.

Don't dwell on them, don't give them life,
But use them as a tool.
If ever again you have the urge to roam
Please, don't be a fool!

Recall the past; prioritize;
Determine what is real.
Make certain if you stray again
You're sure of what you feel.

Make a choice that you can live with,
There won't be another chance.
Listen carefully to the music,
Before you choose to dance!

Distortion

Why do I keep offering solutions?
Why am I suggesting change?
Why do I keep apologizing for my actions?
I'm not the one to blame!

I'm not the one who cheated.
I'm not the one who strayed.
I'm the one that was left behind
When you decided to go out to play.

You're the one who had the pleasure.
You're the one who chose to leave.
Now, I'm the one who has to cope;
I'm the one who grieves!

Silence

I can see that you're exhausted.
Emotions take their toll.
My instinct is to help you heal,
To try to ease your soul.

But you brought this upon us.
You made a conscious choice!
And though I know my words might help,
I will not give them voice!

Changes

You opened your arms, you closed your heart,
You changed our whole way of life.
You expanded your work, you forgot about home,
You forgot about having a wife!

Did the sound of her voice, the caress of her lips,
Cause your spirits and heartbeat to soar?
Did your time spent with her and the feel of her arms
Leave you constantly longing for more?

Did you just float along with a new zest for life
That you hadn't realized for years?
Did you feel more of a man than ever before
'Til your happiness drowned in my tears?

Did I take away something special from you?
Do you long to be back in her bed?
Do you look at me daily and swallow regret;
So sorry that we ever wed?

My heart has been broken, it may never heal,
It's been trampled by so many schemes!
Go with my blessings; and deep, deep remorse;
You're free to follow your dreams.

Memories

How often do you miss her voice;
Her lips, her eyes, her hair?
How often do you reach for me;
Wishing, she were there?

How sorry are you for letting her go?
How often do you yearn?
Are you sorry you chose to settle for me?
Does your passion for her still burn?

Do you think you'll ever forget her?
Do you think we'll ever be free?
Do you think you'll ever be happy again?
Content with only me?

The Substitute

The crowning achievement of my whole life,
Was that I had married you!
I wore my ring with honor and pride
Each day the whole day through.

I believed in our love and our marriage.
I believed in our sacred trust.
I had no idea I was performing a job,
That there really was no "us!"

I thought I was your soul mate.
I took to heart all that you said.
I had no idea I was a stand by,
While others shared your bed!

You lost the need to talk to me.
You no longer seemed to care.
You preferred to talk with someone else.
You found another with whom to share.

You shared your time and attention,
You shared your body as well.
You destroyed a loving marriage.
You created a resounding knell!

DISTRUST

Patience

Send her flowers; she's shallow;
She'll accept them with a smile on her face.
Tell her more lies; she's gullible;
She'll listen with a woman's grace.

Throw her a bone; she deserves it;
After all she's been there for years!
Turn a deaf ear when she's angry;
Ignore her; it's only her fears.

Tell her that you're really sorry!
That it will never happen again!
Then as soon as she is settled;
You can go out and find a new friend!

The Enemy

You've hurt me far beyond my words.
I don't know how I'll heal.
I try so hard to move ahead,
To deal with what's now real.

I try to overcome the past,
I try to let it go!
But painful thoughts assail me;
They've become my greatest foe!

They take my very breath away,
They cause my eyes to tear.
They've stolen my security;
I live each day in fear!

I'm so afraid you'll cheat again
I quake at just the thought;
You've no idea, the awful pain,
Your thoughtless actions brought!

Voices

Those women you chose to be with?
The ones you took to your bed?
You tell me you no longer see them;
Well I do; they live in my head!

They laugh when you say you're sorry!
They whisper you'll never be true.
They tell me to just tend my duties;
They're out there waiting for you.

They tell me that they can be patient;
You're certainly well worth the wait!
As soon as my grieving is over;
You'll be calling to set up a date.

CIRCLES

Valleys

My life's a roller coaster,
I'm up and then I'm down.
A thought, a word, a gesture,
Can turn a smile to a frown.

The pinnacles of the mountains
Make the valleys seem so deep.
Anger, fear, depression,
All keep me from my sleep.

I try to face each day anew,
To make the smiles last,
But an ache is constant in my heart;
I can't escape the past!

The anguish I feel is endless;
I cannot purge the pain!
I pray someday I'll learn to cope;
I'll learn to trust again.

Devastation

It began with shock and disbelief,
Then turned to sobs and wrenching grief.

My tears would flow at just a thought,
My quests for ease were all for naught.

Grief changed to rage that ruled my days,
Engulfing most nights in a bitter haze.

As time marched on, my anger lessened.
Restful nights, brought dawns re-freshened.

Pain would come, and tears would flow,
Fear was constant, and healing slow.

No Answers

Like a carousel horse,
I'm up; then I'm down.

I move to the music
Going 'round and around.

I make no progress;
I gain no ground.

I keep seeking answers
Where none can be found!

Escape

There are days I'd like to run away.
I revel in the thought!
I'd run away from memories
And all the pain they've wrought.

I'd run away from daily ghosts;
I'd run away from doubt.
I'd leave behind the awful fears
I can't seem to live without.

I'd forget about betrayals;
I'd leave behind the lies.
I'd just run ever onward;
And forget your artful guise!

Second Best

I don't want to be negative!
I don't want to leave!
But I get so damned tired
Of having to grieve!

I hope in my heart
The pain will soon end!
I pray you'll be true
And not seek a new "friend!"

But none of that stops
The thoughts from intruding;
No amount of reason
Can keep me from brooding!

I am stabbed by the facts
That can't be denied!
I sometimes drown in the memory
Of the tears I have cried!

I revisit actions!
I get hung up on phrases!
I question intents!
I distrust all your praises!

My mind's like a razor,
My heart becomes lead
As I go over, and over,
All the words in my head!

For years you deceived me;
All my memories are false!
You kept me on the sidelines
While you continued to waltz!

Stuck

I've written poems to say goodbye,
I've said I've learned my lesson.
I've tried so hard to walk away;
But my heart just would not listen!

I've heard the pretty words you speak,
I'm stunned by all your actions!
I've counted on your promises,
But got no satisfaction!

I've tried to let the past be past,
I've tried to keep things light;
Yet visions haunt me daily
And still keep me up at night.

The Battlefield

Every day is a constant battle,
It's a struggle to keep my mind clear.
To keep my thoughts in the present,
To suppress my burgeoning fear.

Bitter memories can quickly engulf me,
Leaving me breathless and weak.
Enslaving me with their power,
Never providing the answers I seek.

Timing

A fist is clenching at my heart,
The sensation leaves me weak.
Harsh memories surround me,
The outcome seems so bleak!

I made myself a promise,
A few short years ago,
That if a feeling came upon me,
I would not let it go!

For years I tried to write one off,
For years I was deceived!
In the future I won't play the fool,
My feelings I'll believe!

I'll walk away, I'll pack it in!
I won't suffer so again.
But now that push has come to shove,
How do I know just when?

When do I trust that feeling?
When do I say goodbye?
When do I give up all I love?
When do I start to cry?

TRAPPED

Cycles

The anger will pass,
The fear will begin.
The shame will set in;
I just can't win!

Your lies will resound,
My grief will abate.
Your patience will die;
It will be too late!

Dawning

I think I finally understand;
I have to let you go.
But how I'll find the strength to leave,
Is something I don't know!

You brought me so much happiness,
You made me feel so fine,
It's so damned hard to live with you
And know that you're not "mine."

I'm sorry I can't share you,
I'm selfish with my pleasures,
I just won't be your "back-up"
When you are all I treasure!

Decisions

Part of me says; don't let this go!
It was far too great of a sin!
Part of me says; let the past be the past!
It's a battle I just can't win!

If I try to move on, will you think it's okay,
To have another affair?
If I put it behind me, and offer my trust,
Will you handle my heart with care?

I know I can't change what has happened to us;
I don't know if I can forgive.
But I must decide what to do with my life;
To determine how I want to live.

Exposed

Anger and resentment,
Self-loathing mixed with dread;
A recipe for suicide
Within a lesser head!

A total lack of discipline,
No inner motivation;
A quick escape to fantasy
To mask the deprivation.

No outer source of happiness,
No inner sense of pride;
Just an angry, lonely woman
Without a place to hide.

Friends

Grief, Fear and Gratitude
Have become my closest friends.
They are with me every moment,
Their presence never ends.

Grief is sometimes quiet
As she lurks within the dark;
Fear is often active
Stabbing at my heart.

Gratitude's persistent
And ever at my ear
Pointing out my status
Threatening me with Fear.

She says I'd best be mindful
And be grateful for your love
Or once again you'll walk away
And Grief will rise above.

Forsaken

I've thrown out the mementos
That represented my beliefs.
I've tried to face reality,
I've searched for some relief.

I've tried to assess my feelings
To determine where I stand.
I've tried to keep in step with you,
To travel hand in hand.

I've tried to fill your every need;
I've tried so hard to please;
Some days are just not worth it;
I only want to leave!

The mementos may be out of sight,
But the beliefs still clench my heart!
It's so damned hard to move ahead
When we think so far apart!

There are days when grief assails me,
There are nights filled with regret.
I try to overcome my fears,
I try to just forget!

Yet, I can't get past your patterns!
Your overwhelming control!
I can't forget what I've compromised;
That I've sacrificed my soul.

Impatience

Have you tired of my sorrow?
Can you no longer bear my pain?
Are you thinking of your old ways?
Would you like to cheat again?

Does your promise to be faithful
Go against your very core?
Would you rather have your freedom?
Would you rather have your whore?

I won't settle for a piece of you,
So please make your decision.
I will learn to live without you;
I can deal with your excision!

Impressions

I watch you pass my window,
I note your steady stride.
I'm reminded of my heartache,
Of all the tears I've cried.

I see arms that held other women;
Other husband's wives.
I see lips that kissed and savored;
Lips that changed my life.

I see a set of shoulders
That sloughed away my fears,
That cared not for the pain I felt
As I shed my tears.

Muscles

The heart, they say, is all muscle;
It should be strong from constant use.
Mine, however, is weakened;
It's withstood too much abuse!

The tongue is also a muscle;
Lately mine is too strong to hold,
Often lashing away from my good sense,
Saying things better left untold!

Shifting Sands

Our marriage was my stability.
Your honesty was my truth.
My life was strong and centered,
Your love provided proof.

The earth was firm beneath me.
I was strong, I had no fears.
Now I find there was no substance,
It had been sand for several years!

Sand that shifts and settles.
Sand that prospers grief.
Sand that affords no foundation.
Sand that supports no belief.

Starting Over

Would I be better off alone?
Would this pain be easier to face?
If I left our home; left our life;
Just vanished without a trace?

My life's been a lie for some time now.
It hurts to face the truth.
It will be harder now to start over
I no longer have my youth.

If I leave, will the daily reminders,
Stay behind with my broken heart?
Or will they just travel with me;
Deterring me from a fresh start.

The Debt

Whatever I did to deserve this,
I pray the debt has been paid!
The payback has been overwhelming!
My nerves are totally frayed!

I don't trust any words, any gestures,
I no longer know which way to turn.
If this is to be my lesson in life,
I hope there's not much more to learn!

The Fog

Life offers no guarantees,
Nor does love and marriage.
Make your own way; walk if you must;
Don't await a carriage.

Take what you get; give what you can;
Always do your best.
Look for answers within yourself,
Someday there'll be a test.

Study hard; store sweet words,
Hope they don't turn sour!
Smile a lot! Love yourself!
Remember, life's a flower.

Flowers need both sun and rain,
Either can be too much.
You must create a balance,
Develop a nurturing touch.

If you're always in the sun
Over time you will be burned;
The rain will come in torrents
With each new lesson learned.

For several years I basked in sun,
It left me weak and frail.
Now I'm lost within a fog;
Fraught with stark betrayal.

The Keeper

I allowed you to be my healer.
I demanded you soothe my soul.
Now I've become dependent on you,
Once again, you have control!

I turned to you for my comfort,
I looked to you for ease.
Now I'm locked within myself
And you hold all the keys.

Unforgiven

Given too much time to think,
My mind resents my heart!
I rue the choices made for love,
Instead of what was smart!

I wrestle with the logic,
I struggle with the pain.
I worry for the future,
I crumble from the strain.

I don't like the weakened person
I've allowed myself to be;
I don't like the woman in the glass,
That stares back out at me!

Visions

Hey, you! With the red eyes; in the mirror.
Hey, fool, staring back out at me!
How many more times, will you fall for his lies,
Before you'll be able to see?

To see, he's not yours! Never has been!
To see, he needs more than you give?
To see, he'll keep changing his story?
'Til it fits with the way that you live!

Ask a question; he'll give you an answer.
Ask again; he'll answer anew.
If you hurt, he'll be quick with assurance
That he's changed; he's going to be true!

He'll be true alright! To his instincts!
And those don't include your beliefs!
He'll be true to his basic desires,
Which will cause you more heartache and grief!

You want to stay? Then stay for a while.
But realize that you have lost!
He'll say whatever it takes to keep you;
Will you stay regardless of cost?

It will cost you your pride and your values!
What else will you give away?
Ask yourself; is he worth all the trouble?
And the pain you will have if you stay!

Wonderful

You tell me that I'm wonderful!
You tell me that you care.
You tell me that you love me
With a love beyond compare.

My mind can't grasp the concept
While my heart still twists in pain,
But I try to find the truth I need
To bring me peace again.

While I'd like to just accept your words,
They beg a definition.
So after much provoking thought
I'll offer my rendition …

W stands for "**workhorse**"
My capacity is vast.

O is "**one**" and "**only**"
You needn't worry 'bout my past!

N is for "**naivety**"
I believe all that you say.

D demonstrates my "**devotion**"
It never goes away.

E stands for "**equality**"
That which I don't receive,

R depicts the "**regret**" I feel
For no more dreams to weave.

F is my "**fidelity**"
As constant as the seasons.

U for "**understanding**"
Acceptance of the reasons.

L is for the "**love**" I give
As natural as my breathing;

WONDERFUL ~ your word of choice
That often finds me grieving!

Vanished

The woman that I thought I was
Is gone forevermore.
I've shattered into pieces,
I'm damaged to the core!

I've no idea what deed I did
That caused this retribution,
But I pray the lesson's over,
That it's come to its fruition!

FORGIVENESS

Accounting

Your actions have become my payback.
My thinking must be reset.
There are so many things to remember;
There are so many things to forget!

I need to remember my missteps
When my heart constricts with grief;
They must be weighed with your failures
If I want a sense of relief.

Only I can deal with my demons;
Only I can purge this pain;
Only I can balance the ledgers,
And achieve inner peace again.

New Beginnings

I sat last night and re-read the poems
I'd written because of you.
I recoiled from the sorrow I'd felt
Because you were not true.

My writing helps purge the poisons
That constrict my heart in pain.
My poems help create a platform
On which I can build again.

My words once put on paper
Help rid me of the past,
Freeing me to move forward,
Allowing a new die to be cast.

The New Chapter

It's time for a new chapter,
It's time for a new song.
The past has all been written,
You cannot right the wrong.

It's time to move us forward,
It's time to redefine.
It's time for you to ask yourself;
Are you ready to be mine?

I won't settle for a portion,
In the future I won't share.
I can learn to live without you!
Push me if you dare!

I'd prefer to stay beside you,
If you want I'll step aside,
But I will not be a number!
I still have a little pride.

I will learn to trust my instincts.
I will be much more alert.
I will learn again to trust you.
You must learn you cannot flirt.

Ya, But

Ya, but.........gets me nowhere!
Ya, but.........causes pain!
Ya, but.........is not helpful!
Ya, but.........brings the rain.

I'd rather have the sunshine!
I'd rather look ahead.
I'd rather feel elation,
Than face each day with dread.

I cannot change what's over.
I can't erase the past.
I can enjoy your presence;
I can pray that it will last.

I can revel in your goodness;
Or I can dwell upon your harm.
I can wallow in self-pity
Or find comfort in your arms.

Each day's about our choices;
We make them every 'morn;
We can seek to find our happiness
Or dwell within our scorn.